To: Mom

From: Elle

true love

—Two African elephants

South American hyacinth
macaws lovingly groom each other
at the entrance to their nest.

true love

24 surprising stories of animal affection

Rachel Buchholz

NATIONAL GEOGRAPHIC

WASHINGTON, D.C.

Published by the National Geographic Society

ISBN: 978-1-4262-1036-5

The National Geographic Society is one of the world's largest nonprofit scientific and educational organizations. Founded in 1888 to "increase and diffuse geographic knowledge," the Society's mission is to inspire people to care about the planet. It reaches more than 400 million people worldwide each month through its official journal, *National Geographic,* and other magazines; National Geographic Channel; television documentaries; music; radio; films; books; DVDs; maps; exhibitions; live events; school publishing programs; interactive media; and merchandise. National Geographic has funded more than 10,000 scientific research, conservation and exploration projects and supports an education program promoting geographic literacy.

For more information, visit www.nationalgeographic.com.

National Geographic Society
1145 17th Street N.W.
Washington, D.C. 20036-4688 U.S.A.

For information about special discounts for bulk purchases, please contact National Geographic Books Special Sales: ngspecsales@ngs.org

For rights or permissions inquiries, please contact National Geographic Books Subsidiary Rights: ngbookrights@ngs.org

Interior design by Elisa Gibson

Printed in China

12/CCOS/1

Dedicated to
my true love, Joe

*Two young
Tukidale lambs*

introduction

When I was 12, a big, black mutt followed me home from swim practice. My parents reluctantly allowed "Dally" to stay—outside. That clearly wasn't what he had in mind. From the yard, Dally would follow me from room to room, scratching at the windows and barking if he couldn't see me. None too pleased, my parents told me I had to give him up. But guess who came back a few days later? Somehow Dally escaped from the animal shelter, made his way across town, and returned to me.

I thought about Dally when I first read the story of Jake the duck, who waddled eight miles to return to his love, Jemima. As executive editor of *National Geographic Kids*, I constantly read stories of amazing animal devotion. These tales are extremely popular, and it's easy to see why: If animals can show kindness and love, surely humans can as well. Some scientists are skeptical that animals love as people do. But after reading these stories, you might think differently. And I, for one, know in my heart that the first boy truly devoted to me was a big, black dog named Dally.

Rachel Buchholz

Brothers
& Sisters

During their first 12 weeks of life, puppies look to their siblings to learn how to play and socialize.

her brother's keeper

When Stacy Corbin, a fishing guide in Alaska, observed a young male grizzly bear trying to catch salmon, he was worried. Grizzlies probe river bottoms with their front feet until they feel a fish, pin it down, and grab it with their teeth. But a hunter had killed this bear's mother and shot her cub in the foreleg, and the young grizzly was left nearly helpless. Because of his injury, he was only scattering the salmon. Without help, the grizzly would die. But then Corbin saw the bear's sister snag six salmon and drop them at his feet. "She fed him for weeks," Corbin says. "He wouldn't have made it without her." Normally a female bear her age would've gone off on her own, but she chose to stay by her brother's side and help him eat until he was strong enough to feed himself.

Tussling grizzly
bear cubs

*The Chihuahua triplets
and their wheels*

lean on me

Being born different can be hard, but loving family members make life seem easier. Luckily, Carmen, Venus, and Pablo have each other to help cope with their disability. The triplet Chihuahuas were born without their front legs, but these little pups thrived with each other's support. With help from volunteers at the North Shore Animal League America in Port Washington, New York, they exercised in a pool to strengthen their leg muscles and learned to use carts that act as front legs. "Today they can walk like people, hop like kangaroos, and move like dogs in their carts," says Donna Imhof, who adopted the pups. But they're still there for each other, holding bones or cleaning one another's ears. Carmen, Venus, and Pablo didn't let their disability get in the way of living—in fact, it may have helped these siblings become a stronger family.

For there is no
friend like a sister
In calm or stormy
weather.

CHRISTINA ROSSETTI

poet

*Spending all their time together, raccoon
kits never leave the den during the first
two months of their lives.*

*Top-Notch and Foster
in the open water*

stuck like glue

The orcas living off the coast of Vancouver Island exhibit an unusual behavior: The males often stay with their mothers for their whole lives. "They're such social animals they can't live alone," says Naomi A. Rose, a marine mammal scientist. Besides being caretakers, the mothers make sure the rambunctious young males behave. The problem is, when a mother dies, unrelated female orcas want nothing to do with an orphaned adolescent male. So with no one to care for him, the young male often dies, too. It looked like that was going to be the fate of an orca named Foster, who was suddenly alone after his mother died. But then his older brother, Top-Notch, took control. Top-Notch cared for Foster like a protective big brother, swimming side by side with him for ten years. By sticking together, these brothers thrived even after they lost their mother.

a helping hand

Good big brothers never pick on their sisters. *Really* good big brothers use their size, strength, and smarts to *help* their sisters. That's just what a captive bonobo named Kanzi did for his sister, Panbanisha. As part of their enrichment at the Great Ape Trust of Iowa, the two apes would smack one rock against another to make a tool sharp enough to open a food box. Bigger and stronger, Kanzi had no problem making his "knife." "He could more quickly make one that cuts the first time," says William Fields, the center's former director of bonobo research. But Panbanisha struggled. She once reached for her brother's tool, but the observing scientist told her no—she had to make her own. So the brother and sister teamed up. Kanzi secretly hid his knife where Panbanisha could find it. Soon she did, and got inside the food box—
thanks to help from her brother.

Siblings Kanzi
and Panbanisha

There is a little
boy inside the man
who is my brother
...Oh, how I hated
that little boy.
And how I love
him too.

ANNA QUINDLEN
author

*Giant pandas are generally solitary
and will strike out on their own by the
time they are two years old.*

sisters in style

If you have to share a room with your sister, you'd better be able to compromise on how your room is set up. Asha and Min, two Asian small-clawed otters, definitely did. While living at the National Zoo in Washington, D.C., the two were known for rearranging their enclosure several times a day. "We called them our decorators. Min would move some bedding to a high nesting box, then Asha would go right behind her and move the bedding to a box on the floor," says animal keeper Tallie Wiles. Eventually all the bedding would be in one box, and that's where they'd agree to sleep. Asian small-clawed otters are actually known for having tight sibling bonds, curling up in big balls to sleep and tossing rocks back and forth in a game of catch. "If Asha and Min were separated, they'd start calling for each other," Wiles says. "They were extremely close."

Cuddling Asian
small-clawed otters

Snoozing piglet Wiggles alongside his puppy brothers and sisters

adopt-a-pig

Blended families that bring together step- or adopted siblings aren't unusual in our modern world. Most of the time, families accept new brothers and sisters, no matter where they came from—even when the new sibling is a pig. When Wiggles was born on a farm in Kansas, her owner needed to give her away, so she went to live with a litter of newborn puppies. Wiggles soon adapted to the puppies' lifestyle, and her new siblings accepted her as part of their family. Her brothers and sisters play-wrestled with her, snuggled with her at night, and even nursed alongside her. Wiggles soon started thinking of herself as a pooch, preferring dog chow over pig food. "She'd even nibble on us like a puppy would," says owner Nellie Davis. When it came to family, these guys didn't see dogs and pigs—they saw only brothers and sisters.

We were a strange little band of characters trudging through life sharing diseases and toothpaste...loving, laughing, defending, and trying to figure out the common thread that bound us all together.

ERMA BOMBECK
humorist

Seldom at a loss for playmates, an arctic fox can have as many as 13 siblings in its litter.

Parents
&
Caregivers

Polar bear moms may nurse their cubs for as long as three years.

to the rescue

A terrified lion cub had tumbled off a ledge and was clinging to a sheer cliff wall in Kenya's Maasai Mara Game Reserve. He was slipping closer to the river below, where he might become prey for a crocodile. His mother started to creep down the slope, but it was too steep and she retreated. "Both seemed terrified, but neither knew what to do," says Jean-François Lagrot, a wildlife photographer who shot the ordeal. The mother lion didn't give up. She headed back down and used her strong paws to grasp the wall as she edged closer to her cub. Just as he lost his strength, she swooped underneath him, grabbed the scruff of his neck with her mouth, and clawed back up the ledge. The mother comforted her cub with some motherly licks on the head. She had come to his rescue—as any mother would do for her child.

Holding her cub in her mouth, the mother lion scales the cliff wall.

Rosie the manatee (left) and Electra, one of her charges

go tell Aunt Rosie

All children need a favorite aunt, someone who loves them without judgment in a way a parent sometimes can't. At Homosassa Springs Wildlife State Park in Florida, that aunt is Rosie, a manatee that's been living at the park since 1980. Affectionately called Aunt Rosie by keepers, the manatee has taken more than 20 young ones under her flipper, whether they were orphans or simply in need of a babysitter. She's been known to nurse orphan calves (even though she's never raised her own) and to assist when these endangered mammals need to float to the surface for air. Once, when an injured young manatee named Electra couldn't float, Rosie let the manatee rest on her back till she was better. Rosie is there for her calves whenever they need her, but just like a true aunt, she also seems to know when to back off gently and let them be themselves.

Having a child is surely the most beautifully irrational act that two people in love can commit.

BILL COSBY
comedian

Falkland steamer ducks will follow their parents, who mate for life, in a line, but they won't take wing; these ducks are flightless.

Watchful Mabel and
her brood of puppies

mother hen

Nettle, a mother dog, never worried when she needed a break from her pups. A chicken named Mabel was happy to take over as surrogate mom. Brought to live inside a farmhouse in England after a horse stepped on her foot, Mabel would fluff up her feathers, plop down on top of her brood of pups, and tuck them under her body as if they were chicks. She'd cluck softly to her "hatchlings" and comfort them till Nettle returned. And though she would allow the puppies to paw at her feathers, Mabel knew when to teach them a valuable lesson about playing nice. "Sometimes if they got too rough, Mabel gave them a gentle peck," farmer Edward Tate says. It's in a chicken's nature to sit on anything warm and nestlike. But Mabel may have had another side to her nature—a strong maternal instinct.

sea of love

The sea otter mother was going hunting off the California coast. Like most mother otters do, she secured her pup in sea kelp to keep him safe while she was away. But a surge of seawater unleashed while she was hunting, tore the pup from the kelp, and washed him away. The pup was in grave danger. How could his mother find him, lost at sea? Suddenly she heard her pup's faint cries. She raced after them until she came to a power plant. Her pup had been sucked into an intake tunnel, and rescuers from the Marine Mammal Center near San Francisco were trying to help. The mother waited by the water's edge until the rescuers returned her wailing pup, frightened but unharmed. "He climbed right up on her chest," rescuer Michael Coffman says. Because of the sea otter's determination, mother and pup were reunited, able to swim as a family once again.

An otter pup balances on his mother's belly.

Life affords no greater responsibility,
no greater privilege, than the raising
of the next generation.

C. EVERETT KOOP, M.D.

physician

*Highly social, two or three meerkat families live together,
and all the members help to care for the young.*

a rockin' dad

Some parents will do anything to have a child. This flamingo was so dedicated to becoming a dad that he tried to hatch a rock. Male and female flamingo pairs, which usually mate for life and raise chicks together, take turns warming their eggs until they hatch. But Andy, a flamingo that lives at the Wildfowl and Wetlands Trust in England, sat on an egg-shaped stone. Nigel Jarrett, head of conservation breeding at the wetlands, thinks that the real egg was knocked from the nest into the water. Then the bird may have mistaken an egg-shaped stone buried in his nest for the egg. "When he saw it, he probably did what any other expectant daddy flamingo would do—he sat on it!" Jarrett says. The flamingo stayed with his adopted egg for two days until he caught on. His egg may have been fake, but Andy's devotion was definitely real.

Andy the flamingo and his "egg"

A baby African elephant rests at his mother's side.

a family affair

The baby elephant was trapped. After stumbling into a dried-up mud hole in Amboseli National Park in Kenya, the calf was too little to climb back up the steep slope to safety. His mother, Round Ears, ran into the hole to help. But now what? She bellowed, attracting the attention of two relatives that rushed over and stepped into the pit. That's when biologist Cynthia Moss observed a scene that showed the strong, loving bond shared among elephant families, as well as the animals' unusual intelligence. The three adults started digging out one side of the hole with their tusks and feet as they built a ramp of dirt. As soon as they finished, Round Ears pressed her head against the calf's rump and pushed her baby up the now-manageable slope. "Elephants are very cooperative," Moss says. Sometimes, it seems, it's a good thing to have a herd mentality.

I don't remember who said this, but there really are places in the heart you don't even know exist until you love a child.

ANNE LAMOTT
author

Mother donkeys and their foals share a strong bond. Foals are weaned when they are about six months old or when the next foal is born.

Best
Friends

Thriving on companionship, dogs form strong social bonds with each other through play.

I've got your back

Agonizing bleats pierced the air. A sheep named Stanley had been quietly munching on grass near his barn in England when a runaway pit bull attacked him. The dog sank his teeth into the sheep's side and wouldn't let go. Dotty, an orphaned donkey who had lived with Stanley since a few years earlier, heard the cries for help and raced to her friend. With no regard for her own life, Dotty charged the dog. "She just sprang into action," owner Ann Rogers told a local reporter. "She jumped off the bank she was on and with a screech of rage pinned the dog to the ground." Finally the dog gave up and released Stanley, who was injured but soon recovered from his traumatic experience. Donkeys are protective by nature, but the story of Dotty demonstrates just how far some animals will go to protect their friends.

Stanley the sheep and
Dotty the donkey

Samantha the gorilla and Panda the rabbit

some bunny to love

Samantha, a western lowland gorilla, had always been something of a loner. The only "friend" she had at the Erie Zoo in Pennsylvania was a stuffed toy gorilla, which she carried around like a treasured doll. Then zookeepers introduced Samantha to a rabbit named Panda. At first the two animals got used to each other through a mesh screen, and slowly they became friends. Eventually, Panda would sit peacefully at the gorilla's feet, and Samantha would stroke Panda's back and scratch her under the chin. Once Panda came upon Samantha's stuffed "baby," which was blocking her way. Keepers worried the gorilla would aggressively protect the toy from the rabbit, but instead Samantha pushed it out of Panda's path. "I'm not sure Panda has replaced the doll in Samantha's heart," says zoo CEO Scott Mitchell, "but they might be equally important to her soon."

What is a friend?
A single soul
dwelling in two
bodies.

ARISTOTLE
philosopher

*Living with humans for some 9,000
years, pigs cooperate in social
groups known as sounders.*

friends forever

When Tarra the elephant and Bella the dog met at the Elephant Sanctuary in Tennessee, they quickly formed a close friendship. Bella trusted the 8,700-pound elephant so much that she let Tarra rub her belly with her trunk. When Bella fell ill, caretakers carried Bella outside so the two animals could be in contact with each other. "Bella and Tarra gave each other unconditional love 24/7," says sanctuary cofounder Carol Buckley. But later, tragedy struck: Bella was found dead, presumably killed by coyotes. Strangely, no evidence of an attack—tufts of hair, bloodstained grass—was found near her body. Keepers did, however, find blood on the underside of Tarra's trunk—as if she had carried her friend home from the fatal encounter. No one knows for sure if this really happened, but one thing is true: Tarra honored her best friend till the end.

Tarra the elephant and Bella the dog

*Bear the bobcat grooms
Robi the caracal.*

grumpy old men

Bear the bobcat was mean, friendless, alone, and nearly blind. Staff at WildCat Haven in Oregon knew he needed a friend, but what cat would put up with him? Enter Robi, an equally grumpy caracal. Keepers moved the two next to each other in the hope they'd bond over their surliness. Soon Bear started rubbing against the fence that separated them and cooing at Robi as the caracal showed off some friendly tail swishing. After keepers opened the fence, the two cats were soon lying in the sun together while the purring bobcat kneaded Robi's fur. Over time the friendship deepened. When Bear completely lost his sight, Robi stepped in as a sort of guide cat, walking just a nose length ahead to steer the bobcat. "Bear is so reliant on Robi," says Cheryl Tuller, sanctuary cofounder. "Robi takes that as his job."

The friend who holds your
hand and says the wrong thing
is made of dearer stuff than the
one who stays away.

BARBARA KINGSOLVER
author

*Chimpanzees are social animals that help each other out. For instance, they
will give away tools without requiring immediate reciprocation.*

A leaping bottlenose dolphin. A surfacing false killer whale (opposite)

bustin' loose

At Sea Life Park Hawaii, Keiki, a bottlenose dolphin, had a tank right next to his pal Ola, a false killer whale (a large member of the dolphin family). At night, Keiki would leap over the fence separating their tanks so the two could play together in Ola's pool. Train-  ers tried placing a plank on top of the fence to make it difficult for Keiki to jump over. But when they arrived the next morning, the plank was in the water—and the dolphin was in Ola's tank. A sneaky trainer finally spied the false killer whale standing on his tail and pushing off the plank with his nose so Keiki could visit. "They'd never do it when we were around," said behavioral biologist Karen Pryor. "They knew we'd put them back in their own tanks."

guardian goose

A big Highland bull like Hamish probably doesn't need a bodyguard, but a certain goose seems to disagree. Whenever the bull is in his pasture at Knapdale Eco Lodge in New Zealand, the goose watches for cattle that—in the bird's opinion—get way too close. "Then he'll stretch out his neck, shriek, and chase the other cows and bulls away," says Kees Weytsmans, the lodge's owner. The bird has barely left the bull's side for ten years—ever since he was found resting on Hamish's leg a week after the bull was born. Weytsmans once moved the bull to another rancher's pasture for a few nights, but one evening apart was all the goose could stand. "The next afternoon the goose traveled all by himself to the other pasture to find Hamish," he says. The bull doesn't seem to mind all the attention. Otherwise, Hamish might ruffle some feathers.

*Hamish and his goose
pal hanging out*

When friendships
are real, they are
not glass threads
or frost work, but
the solidest things
we can know.

RALPH WALDO EMERSON

philosopher and poet

*Lions live together in prides that can
be as big as 40 animals.*

Real Romantics

During courtship, mature stallions and mares sniff, nuzzle, nicker, and even nip at each other.

Romeo and Julia with their nest of eggs

return to me

Who says long-distance relationships can't work? A stork named Romeo spends six months every year migrating to and from Africa but always returns to his mate, Julia, who lives in Switzerland. Most male storks fly back to the same nest every year but are happy with any random female that arrives to mate. But when Julia broke her wing and couldn't migrate, she moved into a Swiss zoo and set up her permanent nest there. Now Romeo can't seem to live without her. He returns every March to the zoo and to Julia. When Romeo arrives, Julia gives him a joyful greeting: "She throws her head back and makes a sound with her beak, like clapping," says zoo curator Friederike von Houwald.

Ah, the sounds of true love.

devoted duo

Most dogs don't get to choose their own mates. But when two huskies named Misha and Maria met, they knew they'd be together forever. The first time Misha lay eyes on Maria in the living room of his owner's friend, he leaped over another dog's head to get to her, and they playfully chased each other around until their owners pulled them apart. Later that day Misha's owner took him home, but not for long—Misha found his way back to Maria's house, dug under the fence surrounding the backyard, and let Maria out. The two then embarked on a 24-hour romantic escapade around Peterborough, New Hampshire. But this was no one-night stand. After Maria had her puppies, Misha stepped up as a father figure, throwing up food for his newborn pups to eat, just as a wolf parent would do.

A playfully romping male and a female husky

Love is an irresistible desire to be irresistibly desired.

ROBERT FROST

poet

When looking for love, female cats are quite vocal, making noises that range from soft purrs to loud caterwauls.

*Two devoted
Diana monkeys*

hey, big boy!

Beulah certainly knew how to get what she wanted from her mate, Rocky. At the Oregon Zoo, these two Diana monkeys were given tokens for a vending machine filled with apples, oranges, and bananas. Every day, Beulah sat beside Rocky while he used his tokens to get food and handed it over to her. Only Beulah could eat Rocky's fruit—he would push away offspring vying for the goodies. "But," observed scientist Hal Markowitz, "Beulah never managed to insert [the tokens] on her own." One day, as Beulah struggled with her tokens, Rocky took one and slid it into the machine. Keepers thought he might keep the snack, but instead he gave the treat to his mate. No one knows if Beulah didn't understand how to get the snack, or if perhaps she just wanted some pampering. No matter— it seems Rocky just wanted his love to be happy.

Timmy and the real girl

Sometimes you never know what's going to spark a love connection. A tortoise named Timmy appears to be in love with Tanya, a plastic tortoise. The two have been an item for 20 years, and Timmy has never shown any interest in other tortoises. "They spend their days together," says Joy Bloor, who takes care of the pair. "If Timmy wants to go somewhere, he pushes Tanya along with him." He even tries to share his food by nudging his lettuce toward her. When the pair arrived at a tortoise sanctuary that Bloor used to run, she tried to separate them and put Timmy in with real tortoises. But the other tortoises bit him and chased him away. Now Timmy lives only with Tanya. Maybe it really does take a good woman to get a guy to come out of his shell.

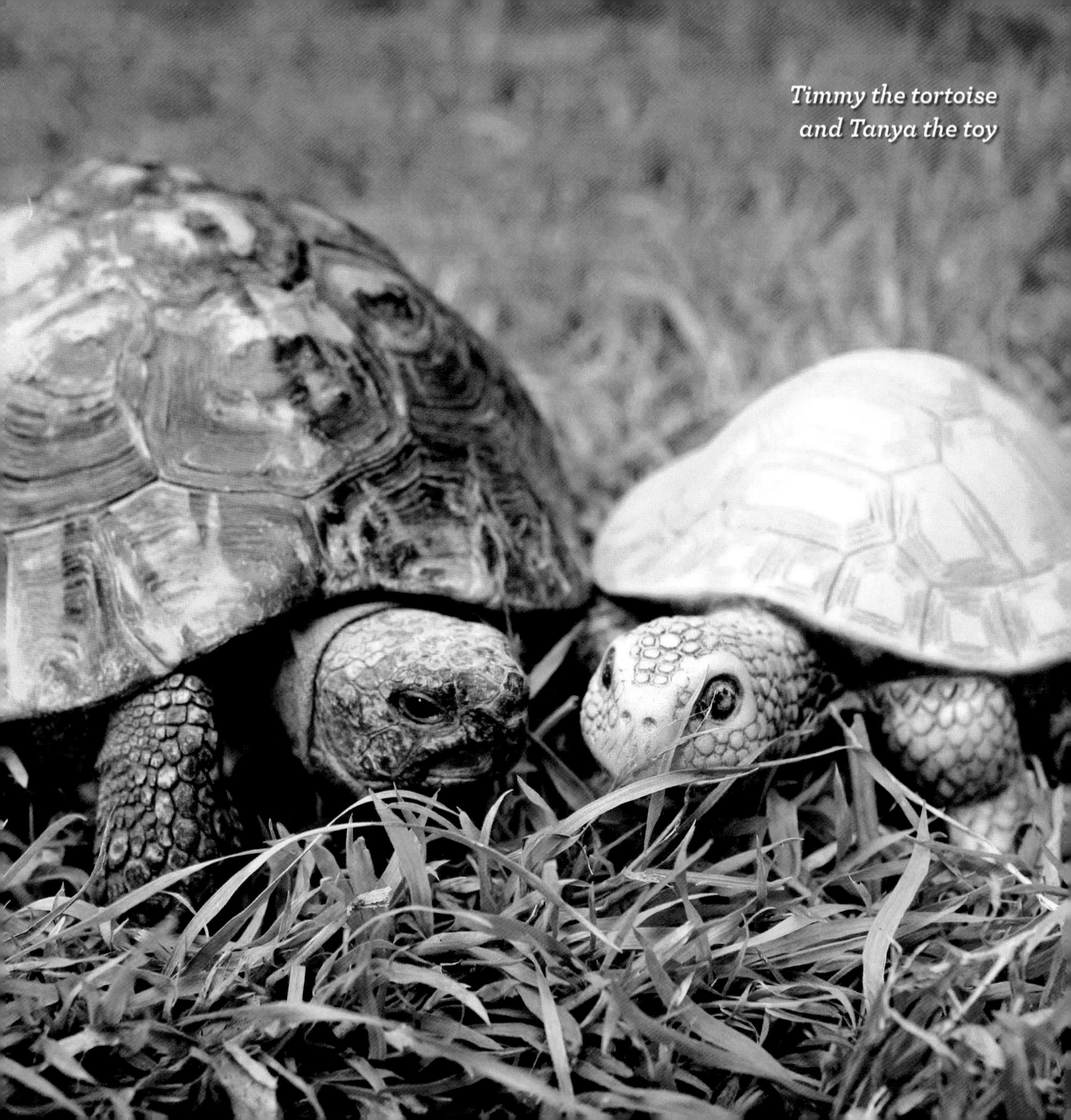

*Timmy the tortoise
and Tanya the toy*

You don't love someone because they're perfect, you love them in spite of the fact that they're not.

JODI PICOULT
author

Harvest mice live in the tall grasses of northern Europe and Asia.
Their nests, made of woven leaves, take a day or two to build.

road to love

Nothing was going to keep Jake and Jemima apart. The two Muscovy ducks had been mates at a farm in England until their owner decided to give Jake to a friend eight miles away. When Jake disappeared, the new owner feared his duck had met a hungry fox. But after Jake turned up a month later at Jemima's home, the owners realized true love was at work. In the weeks while Jake waddled back to Jemima, he weathered three snowstorms, risked animal attacks, and searched for openings through tall hedges he was too chubby to fly over. He also had to navigate through miles of wooded terrain that did not suit his webbed feet. In the end, Jake was allowed to stay with Jemima. "When he came back, they were like an old married couple," says Roy Shindler, the pair's owner.

Sometimes love truly does conquer all.

Jake the Muscovy duck walking down the road

Two white-cheeked gibbons, a dark-furred male (left) and a cream-colored female

perfect harmony

What's a dude to do when he's too shy to tell a girl he likes her? Some guys write songs to express their feelings. That's what Bailey, a white-cheeked gibbon, did for his mate Tia. Extremely shy when he first met Tia at the Minnesota Zoo, Bailey would sit on the opposite side of their enclosure. But then he started to sing. Today, Bailey calls to his mate in a high soprano voice nearly every morning, and Tia responds with a loud whooping noise. "They do this around 8:30 or 9 in the morning, regardless of the time of year or the light," says Tom Ness, tropics curator at the zoo. Now the two seem more bonded; they even pass food such as grapes and biscuits to each other. It may not be the "Greatest Duet of All Time," but for Bailey and Tia, it's the perfect love song.

It is a curious thought, but it is only when you see people looking ridiculous that you realize just how much you love them.

AGATHA CHRISTIE
author

Female moose find irresistible the strong scent exuded by male bulls during the late summer and early fall.

illustrations credits

A pair of
little owls